The Miracle Pr

Fig. 1. Bell Rock is shown to the right (the left formation is Courthouse Butte).

THE MIRACLE PROBLEM-SOLVER

Using crystals and
the power of Sedona
to transform your life

Kira Klenke

EARTHDANCER

A FINDHORN PRESS IMPRINT

Disclaimer

The information in this book is given in good faith and is not intended to diagnose any physical or mental condition or serve as a substitute for informed medical advice or care. Please contact your health professional for medical advice and treatment. Neither author nor publisher can be held liable by any person for any loss or damage whatsoever that may arise from the use of this book or any of the information therein.

Contents

How this book came about

The indigenous people of North America have had a tradition for millennia: when they are seeking a solution to a problem or advice on an urgent, pressing decision, they go out into the natural world with the question in their hearts, to a place where they feel a close connection to the 'Great Spirit' (as they call the source of all being). Here, they tap into the silence within themselves and rely on their intuitive antennae. Reading the signs of Nature (such as cloud or rock formations, encounters with animals or other manifestations that spontaneously appear to them), they interpret a solution and find an answer to the question.

The method outlined in this book works in a similar way – but you can use it just as easily at home.

I first became aware of the SOURCE oracle and constellation method (described here for the first time) many years ago, on a holiday in Native American country in Arizona. The method came to me entirely of its own volition in Sedona, probably one of the most potent power places on the planet. I was sitting on top of the 'Bell Rock', an area of bedrock that emanates unusually strong energy, and had been meditating there and writing in my diary. It was here that I wrote this book.

A letter for you from Arizona

I wrote this letter years ago in Sedona, for you. Yes, you read that right: this letter is indeed for you, the person holding this book in their hands right now.

Sedona, July 2009

Dear friend,

I am writing you this letter from my holiday here in Sedona in Arizona. And I am picturing you, yes *you*, the person reading this book right now, in my mind.

I would like to tell you what I have experienced in the mystical homeland of the Native North Americans over the last few weeks, at a place where the atmosphere, the incredible energetic power and the primeval beauty go beyond anything I have ever seen in any other power place – and I have seen quite a number of power places over the last twenty years.

The landscape here as you see it today has not changed in millions of years. Please don't ask me exactly how it is formed – geology is not my strong point – but nearby is the Grand Canyon, whose unique beauty attracts visits from hundreds of thousands of tourists every year. People from all over the world come here – even if only as a quick stop on a coach trip – to admire the breathtaking beauty and be gripped by the magnificent presence and sublime wonder of Nature. Spiritual seekers from all round the globe often consciously choose the Grand Canyon as the location for their vision quest. By communing with Nature, they hope to find clues to their mission in life, solutions to important issues close to their hearts or the impetus for changes that are about to be made in their lives.

No matter how consciously or unconsciously these visitors seek contact with Nature here, and however briefly they experience it, every one of them is likely to sense the presence of a higher

Fig. 2: The landscape around Sedona with its red rock, sculpture-like formations

power in this place. It is a powerful reminder of how small and insignificant is a human life – a hundred years at most – in comparison with the timeless majesty of Nature.

The place now called Sedona, a location used for vision quests by the Native Americans for many years, is less internationally famous. There is a striking number of art galleries, workshops and art schools and in Sedona you will run into colourful paintings and sculptures inspired by Nature at every turn. Even if you are not an art lover, I am sure you would soon get itchy fingers here and start wondering if you might want to have a go at painting or some other artistic activity.

Plenty of people have already hit upon the business idea of their lives in the almost innumerable power places that surround Sedona in the mountainous world of the Red Rock State Park; Walt Disney, John Wayne, Al Pacino, Orson Welles and Max

Ernst are among those who have sought inspiration and mentally refuelled here. The 'Sedona method', a technique for quickly and successfully banishing unpleasant emotions in a simple way, was also born here. It is now practised all over the world.

There is a proverb, 'God created the Grand Canyon, but He lives in Sedona', and the indigenous Native Americans have known and visited this place for millennia. They consider it an ideal location to find help and seek answers to life's important questions in Nature – but not, however, a place to put down roots. As is so often the case, the Anglo-American settlers ignored this advice and founded the little town of Sedona.

The Native Americans say that this is 'a place of blessing'; we would describe Sedona as a shrine, or a place of pilgrimage. People here say it is a place of regeneration. It is an ideal place to find peace, discover yourself and gather your strength. Indeed, some even claim it is a place to grow younger.

It is a place of healing, that much is certain. I made friends here with a ranger who a year earlier had been threatened with the amputation of her left leg, which she had damaged through smoking. Instead of agreeing to the operation, she moved here from the state of Wisconsin. The first thing she did was to spend a few weeks just living among Nature, bathing several times daily in the Oak Creek River for many days. This is the river that flows through Sedona, and the Apaches ascribe to it the same cleansing and healing abilities as the Indians do to the Ganges. My friend still has her leg to this day. She once showed it to me: it is covered in scars, proper pockmarked craters. She told me that at the time – when she was really at the end of her tether – she devoted herself to this sacred land as her master. This place saved and healed her. I have often been told that spontaneous healing frequently happens here.

The Native Americans used to come here when they needed 'blessings for their journey through life' – because they were sick, for example, or otherwise somehow felt 'stuck' in their lives – and Sedona was also voted the most beautiful landscape in America in 2009. There is one thing of which I am certain: it is a *magical* place. As far as I am concerned, this is the only word that goes some way towards describing my experiences here. Wishes often come true here within hours.

The book you are reading right now simply 'flowed from my pen', with absolutely no conscious effort from me or any intellectual input or exertion on my part. I neither sought nor desired the topic. Although it linked into knowledge I had acquired over decades, I did no more than move my pen over the paper, as if taking dictation. The content arrived and arranged itself entirely under its own steam. It came – and this is how the Native Americans who live here would put it – through the Great Spirit, through the power of the Red Rocks, through the extraordinary energy of the power places here, through this strong presence, through the blessing of this sacred land that is millions of years old. It was as if the words were dictated to me, whispered into my ear or my heart and placed directly under my hand and my pen.

One thing that made me realise this was that I was no longer able to remember the details of what I had written just a few hours after laying down my pen. I had to reread my blue notebook to be able to try out a technique. I was – and still am – essentially a reader of this book, just like you. Even the name of the method, 'SOURCE', was not invented by me. Sitting on the Bell Rock here, I wrote it down in my diary as if it were being dictated to me:

S Sedona stone
O Oracle
U Unity
R Recreating
C Constellation
E Experience

My husband, my travelling companion here, was the first person with whom I shared all this and tried it out. He was extremely sceptical at first, even when I told him about the really magical way in which the name SOURCE, including the explanations for the acronym, had suddenly occurred to me. He initially refused to cooperate when I asked him for help – instead of playing around with stones with me, he wanted to carry on reading. He pointedly went back to his book, but then started in amazement. 'Look!' he cried, pointing to one of the very first sentences: 'Always follow the Source.'

Dear reader, I am glad that you too can now share in such magic through this book. I wish with all my heart that you will have wonderful and powerful experiences with the aid of the SOURCE technique, and may the adventures it brings you heal and strengthen you, helping you to grow to achieve the resplendent greatness that is your birthright.

I am sending you a powerful beam of this magnificent, luminous, transformative Sedona energy!

Kira Klenke

'Learning consists of remembering information that has lived in the soul of mankind for generations.'

Socrates

What is this book about?

The Native American definition of 'medicine'

The North American Indians would describe the SOURCE method as 'medicine', although the word has a much broader meaning in the Native American world view than it does for us. Their definition can help us to be better at helping ourselves in difficult situations in life. For the Native Americans, the term does not refer solely to medication such as an aspirin or an injection for back pain (which is what we usually think of nowadays). In their tradition, anything that helps a person restore themselves to harmony or peace is medicine. Everything that heals body or mind and restores inner equilibrium is medicine.

The Native Americans would often go out into the natural world to find suitable medicine and/or advice that would help them to heal a personal problem, asking their ancestors or spirit or animal guides for aid.

The first step in the process was to make a clear and firm resolution to solve a very specific problem or clear up a certain matter. The Native Americans firmly believed that the Great Spirit would guide and support them, and by Great Spirit they meant the perfect, original, divine power that created everything and lives within everything. It inhabits every person just as it lives in the sky and the clouds, the stars, the sun and the moon, in plants and animals, rivers, lakes, mountains and, of course, in every stone.

What can you expect to gain from the SOURCE method?

The SOURCE method will provide you with your 'medicine', defined as above. The first thing you too will do during a SOURCE session is to make a firm resolution. In all trust, you will hand over your problem and/or your request for guidance to a higher power. Using a SOURCE stone constellation, you will be able to view the contexts and connections within your life with new eyes. You will use your intuition to interpret the signs of the stones and then follow the subtle impulses that lead you in the direction of the solution you seek. By doing this, you will suddenly discover new opportunities you had previously overlooked. A SOURCE session is the start of an energetic harmonisation and healing process guided by the Great Spirit and/or the Source that lies behind all being – when we succeed in linking ourselves to the place from which everything was created, we find the answer to every question and a solution for any problem.

Using the SOURCE method allows you to establish a connection to the Source with remarkable speed. You will find it amazingly easy to draw profound answers directly from the Source, enabling you to receive new and freeing impulses and healing advice for any problematic situation you can think of. A SOURCE session provides a phenomenally simple way of ending personal crises within the shortest possible time. This book can transform your life and anyone can learn this method extremely quickly!

To achieve this, you need only stick to the easy-to-follow steps described in the book. As a rule, working with SOURCE is a pure joy. It is playful and has an immediate fascination for all those who come into contact with it. It has a positive and supportive effect and heals on every level. Even people who usually find it difficult to formulate goals or desires for the future will easily find a clear new direction with a SOURCE session.

The fantastic thing about the method is that you don't (initially) have to be sure of where the heart of a situation or the nub of a problem lies. This is one of the miracles of SOURCE work and the gift given by this oracle work: as you look down at the stone constellations, the deeper connections within the (conflicted) situation will suddenly reveal themselves – all by themselves!

And the best thing about the method is that the stone constellation will use this newly released energy to draw the future you desire – liberated and healed – into your reality, without you needing to consciously devote any further thought to the matter! This is the miraculous part. The actual 'work' in a SOURCE session happens by itself; it is 'done for you'. The only thing you need to do for it to work is to remain relaxed and open, and to trust in the process.

I have tried out and experienced everything you are reading about here many times over the course of the last few years, either alone or with others. I have been endlessly amazed at the power that lies within the SOURCE method – it is a powerful and transformational force that heals and sets free.

Answers from the Source: the clarifying and transformational power of a SOURCE session

The SOURCE method will help you to heal yourself or free yourself from crises. Everything that requires healing in your life is in your own hands – in the truest sense of the words. Step by step, this book will explain to you the powerful technique of stone oracles and constellations. At each stage, you will automatically gain access to deep wisdom and reliable inner guidance.

Yes, there is such a thing as access to the source of deep, universal wisdom, and you can find it for yourself – anyone can. This door will be opened to you when you relax and are ready to relinquish control for the duration of a SOURCE session, and – for a short while – have no wish to achieve anything specific. Instead, you will open yourself up to 'whatever wants to reveal itself to you right now'. When you listen from inside yourself and trust in this process, the inner voice of your heart or soul (some call it intuition, inspiration or the promptings of an angel) will speak to you. This voice, with its valuable advice and gifts, will astound you. As a rule, the voice is amazingly simple, extremely clear and powerfully effective. It always brings healing, and you will almost always feel immediate relief.

A SOURCE session lays bare the logic and coherence intrinsic to any of life's situations, as well as the next step to freedom (there always is one!) that immediately arises from that situation. This all happens and evolves entirely by itself. Follow the steps described in the book, defining the forces at work in your situation and choosing your stones, then cast the stones and make adjustments to the constellation you have created. This will not only transform your stone constellation but also change the life situation you are addressing.

I have used SOURCE stone oracle work again and again, with lots of other people, over the last few years, and we have researched the method and its transformational power together. With this book, I am passing on what we have learned and experienced.

Who is the SOURCE method suitable for?

Anyone can gain access to profound wisdom and inner guidance using the SOURCE method – with absolutely no previous experience! Anyone can draw new inspiration and answers to their problems from the source of the deepest wisdom. As a rule, these are answers that widen your horizons and immediately cast a different and less drastic light on the problem, providing instant hope that the situation can be changed, while at the same time giving practical indications of how that might happen.

Anyone who regularly meditates or has some skills in shamanism or energy work will get the hang of the technique particularly quickly, and the same is true for those who like to commune with Nature –

with trees, for example – or who like to work with Tarot cards, the I Ching or any other oracle method. Anyone who has undergone (family) constellation therapy will also very quickly feel at home with the SOURCE method.

Possible subjects for a SOURCE session

A SOURCE session is just as suitable as a tool for clearing up professional problems as it is for affairs of the heart. It is as effective for clarifying the relationship between a mother and daughter as it is for seeking a suitable life partner. It can also provide enormous support for courses of medical treatment and healing in the event of health problems. A SOURCE session is also suitable as a handy, calming complement to personal or professional projects, from hunting for a suitable terraced house to writing a Master's thesis or publishing a book.

A woman who had been in psychotherapy for years learned to face her fears using the SOURCE method. During her divorce, a female friend of mine was suffering considerable stress from her husband through the unfair division of their shared property. After a SOURCE session, she consistently concentrated only on what was important to her own new future and what gave her power. I can't think of a single problematic situation for which I would not use SOURCE, if only as an additional aid and support.

SOURCE work dissolves mental blocks and crumbles away old beliefs that sabotage progress and are no longer fit for purpose, occasionally even lifting lingering complications from your earlier life such as old vows or promises. It does all this – and it is important to know this and to acknowledge it! – even if you are unaware of these obstacles yourself.

Reliable help
in all of life's situations

Before we go into every last detail of the method, you should have a sense of where this journey is taking you. So let's begin with a short summary of the method and then explore a sample SOURCE session.

The SOURCE method: a summary

1. Get hold of a handful of smallish stones. Gemstones are extremely suitable, but simple pebbles will do just as well.

Fig. 3. Small semi-precious stones of differing colours work well with the SOURCE method

2. Get into the right frame of mind for the SOURCE session by pausing briefly, meditating for a while or saying a short prayer to set the mood. Resolve to entrust yourself to the flow of the process and/or the guidance of the Source. Ask that your rational understanding and your ego* take a back seat for the duration of the SOURCE session and do not get involved.

3. Define your concern and/or problem. Write it down in a few sentences. As best you can for the moment, also jot down a draft of the outcome you wish for instead. This is not absolutely necessary at this point, however, as it will arise automatically from the results of the SOURCE session.

4. Make a list of the people and influences that you see as involved in the matter. These might be, for example, your jealousy, your husband, a will, an illness or being sacked from your job. These are the 'players'. Here, you should concentrate on the most important, as the more players there are, the more complex the SOURCE process tends to be. Even very complicated situations have been solved in a SOURCE session with only five players.

5. Now select a stone for each of these players; this will later represent the player in the stone constellation. Make a note of which stone represents what or whom, either in your list of players or using a photo (as in the example below).

6. Ask for contact with your inner guide. Now, gently but firmly cast the first stone constellation. As you do so, ask that the stone pattern thrown should represent your current situation clearly.

7. Take a photo of the stone constellation you have thrown.

....

* Here, 'ego' means the inner attitudes, firm convictions and stubborn habits that all too often cause our interpretation of events and reactions to life situations to follow the same, tired path.

8. What noticeable features strike you about this constellation? Make a note of these. In this first stage, leave the meaning assigned to each of the stones to one side as much as you can; it can even be helpful if you cannot remember which stones represent which players. In the next step, you will then 'translate' the patterns or structures you have noted down into content-related associations, using your list of players (step 4 above) and the list of stones with which they are associated (step 5 above).

9. Which stones must now be adjusted so that the situation is harmonised or becomes more bearable, agreeable, peaceful or whatever applies to the topic at hand? Proceed gently and thoughtfully, as every individual adjustment to a stone immediately changes its (energy) relationship with all the others.

   After each alteration, first feel what has changed and sense whether the constellation does indeed feel lightened and better. Here it is possible to make an intermediate move as a test and then to replace the stone if the energy is not clearly improved. You can of course refer to the meanings assigned to each of the stones as you do this, but your gut feeling is always more important. Follow your intuition, as well as any spontaneous impulses or 'inspirations'.

   What should be moved or changed, and how, to make the overall picture more ordered, harmonious, pleasant and healing? Here, you can also add a new, additional player if you need to. You will have reached your target constellation when the appearance or the (energetic) feel of this constellation brings you a sense of 'realisation' or considerable relief.

10. Now take a second photo.

11. As a rule, the assigned meaning of the stones (interpreted in terms of their locations and their positions relative to one another) will generate a message from the target constellation – for example, something like: 'My feelings are now at the centre of things.'

Thinking in terms of the meaning of the stones and their associations with the relevant players, formulate the message from your target constellation into a sentence that brings you strength.

12. Work with the two photos (the picture you took of the original stone constellation you cast and the one of your target constellation) for at least seven days. Do this for about three minutes, twice a day. It is particularly good to do this once in the morning, just after waking up, and once in the evening, just before going to sleep.

To achieve this, place the first photo on your left (or hold it in your left hand) and place the second photo beside it to the right (or hold it in your right hand). Now glance briefly at the left-hand photo before quickly shifting your eyes to the right, to the photo of the target constellation, where you should let your eyes rest for a while.

If you like, repeat your target sentence out loud or to yourself as you do this. Repeat this several times: briefly look at the left-hand photo, then shift your eyes to the right to the second picture, lingering there for a longer period of time.

If you have the space for it, you can also leave your target constellation set up for several days so it can continue to have an influence on you.

13. Observe what changes take place in respect of your situation and/or the problem during and after these seven days.

Experiencing SOURCE at first hand: a sample session

The problematic situation

Jane (name changed) is a 60-year-old teacher who is just about to retire. She enjoys painting (and is very good at it) and has set up a studio in her own home. She is young-looking for her age and very vivacious. The only thing that makes her sad is that she has had no life partner since her husband died a number of years ago. She has signed up for several introductions sites on the internet and, for more than two years, has been having occasional dates with men whose profiles seem to match her own. She says that what she has experienced at these meetings has constantly disappointed her; the men have generally been nothing like the description they posted on the web.

What she has found most upsetting is that, up until now, all the men she has met have almost immediately lost interest in her. This has always happened right after she has confidently explained that painting is her passion, for which of course she would need both free time and space. As she says: 'For my partner, I would really like to find a man who is not put off by a self-confident woman, and who is also interested in art, museums and art exhibitions.'

I first explained the process and the working methods of a SOURCE session. We then got into the right mood by listening to the gentle, uplifting music of the Native North American flautist Carlos Nakai for a few minutes. His peaceful yet intense music goes beautifully with SOURCE work. After this, Jane considered what influences are at work in her problem – these then became the 'players' in her SOURCE session.

Her player list was:

No.	Player
1	A suitable life partner for me
2	Me
3	Painting & art
4	My independence
5	Commitment & loyalty
6	Deep affection
7	Beautiful, pleasurable sexuality
8	Financial security
9	Pleasant ways of finding a partner (via the web, small ads, acquaintances, or ?)
10	What is somehow still missing in the search for a partner at the moment?

She then selected the following stones to represent these players in the SOURCE session:

1 Onyx, 2 Agate, grey, 3 Carnelian, banded, 4 Chrysoprase, 5 Sodalite, 6 Moonstone, 7 Rose quartz, 8 Garnet, 9 Clear quartz, 10 Unakite/Epidote-Feldspar

Fig. 4. Allocation of the crystals to Jane's players

Using these, she threw the following stone constellation, which we photographed:

Fig. 5. The constellation cast by Jane

The patterns or positions we noticed here were:
- 2, 4, 9, 8 and 5 are lying in a cluster, with 9 in the centre.
- 8 is lying close by and 2 is a little further away.
- 6, 1 and 7 are lying further away (in an arc).
- 3 is clearly further away.
- 10 fell out of the constellation entirely and ended up under the table.

We first noted these four striking details using this numbering notation. Neither of us could exactly remember what content or associations lay hidden behind the individual stones. At this point in a SOURCE session, this is in fact exactly what is conducive to observing and interpreting the constellation neutrally and wholly objectively.

It was only in the second stage that we incorporated the assigned meaning of the stones:

1. 'Pleasant ways of finding a partner', 'My independence', 'Commitment & loyalty', 'Financial security' and 'Me' are lying in a cluster, with 'Pleasant ways of finding a partner' in the centre, 'Financial security' close by, and 'Me' a little further away.

2. 'Deep affection', 'A suitable life partner for me' and 'Beautiful, pleasurable sexuality' lie further away (in an arc).

3. 'Painting & art' is much further away and is thus certainly not at the centre.

4. 'Whatever is somehow still missing' has fallen away beneath the table: of course it has, it's what's missing! This mirrors the current situation astonishingly precisely.

The path to the target constellation

Jane spontaneously said that she essentially yearned for what the arc of the three stones 'Deep affection', 'A suitable life partner for me' and 'Beautiful, pleasurable sexuality' represented. However, this was currently not at all the focus of her search for a partner. She was currently concentrating – she could confirm this straight away – on looking for a suitable way of being introduced to a partner. And, as she now went on to say, she basically did not trust all those internet forums and ads. Indeed, she even doubted that this path would lead her to her goal and/or to a new life partner.

She was, however, spending a lot of time on it at the moment, unaware of any other approach. With the men she was meeting, she would first send out a few cautious feelers to see if they were in sound financial shape, whether they had honest intentions about entering a solid interpersonal relationship and whether they were emancipated enough for a strong, independent woman. For these reasons, she had previously broken off contact very quickly – or the men had quickly distanced themselves.

While looking at the stone constellation, she thought:
a) that it would probably be sensible to flag up her love of art (which was so dear to her and one of the focal points of her life) much more clearly in her personal description and/or in the first contact emails and telephone conversations – and to move the relevant stone closer towards the centre of the constellation.

b) that she would like to change her focus at future meetings, mainly to explore whether the man in question could fulfil her key criteria

Fig. 6. The path to Jane's target constellation

of 'Deep affection', 'A suitable life partner for me' and 'Beautiful, pleasurable sexuality'. She decided that the arc of these three players should form the centre of her new target constellation, but ought to be combined with the stone that represents herself. The other players, 'My independence', 'Commitment & loyalty' and 'Financial security' should then lie a certain distance away.

She firmly sidelined the focus on 'methods to find a partner' and integrated the 'what's missing' stone (without it being clear what this might be) into the constellation instead. She then randomly selected an additional stone for her future partner; by chance, it happened to be a beautiful, patterned agate. This fitted well, as the stone that represented her was also an agate.

In fig. 6 you can see the constellation that was created.

Jane quickly noticed that this (unexpectedly) didn't feel right. She felt there were simply far too many stones: there were far too many (sometimes very different) influences in this constellation.

As a result, a reduced stone constellation was produced as a target constellation: see next page, fig. 7.

This became Jane's second SOURCE photo, with her and her future partner united in deep affection, suiting one another well and enjoying beautiful, pleasurable sexuality, brought together with the aid of something of which Jane was currently unaware (stone 10 is isolated at the bottom of the photo).

This was the message from Jane's target constellation.

We ended the SOURCE session with a brief moment of calm. Each of us gave thanks silently. Jane's view of her current situation had been transformed astonishingly quickly in this SOURCE session. Instead of viewing her security from a mainly intellectualised and fearful perspective, she would now concentrate on following her heart. Jane's confidence that the yearnings of her heart would, with the aid of higher guidance, lead her to a suitable new partner was boosted by the outcome of this SOURCE session: 'From now on I shall be looking with my heart, and I am sure I will soon find my ideal life partner.'

Fig. 7. Jane's target constellation

She further reinforced this resolve (and her new attitude and confidence) over the following days by working with the two photos (as described in step 12 of the SOURCE summary above).

When we spoke on the telephone a few weeks later, she told me that her dating candidates now included a few really quite acceptable men with whom she could easily imagine having a relationship.

Learning the SOURCE method from scratch

Now that you have an overview and have gained a first impression of how the SOURCE method is applied, I'll explain the technique step by step, in close detail.

The SOURCE stones

You will need about 10 to 12 stones, each with a diameter of about 1–3 cm. It's a good idea for them to be clearly and obviously different in shape, colour or geological type, so decorative stones such as rose quartz, rock crystal, moonstone, fluorite or tiger's eye are ideal. Coloured glass pebbles are also suitable, but perfectly ordinary stones work just as well.

You can start with a handful of small stones like those you might find on a stroll, for example. For SOURCE work, it is useful if the stones can be easily distinguished from each other visually.

If the stones you discover in the natural world prove difficult to tell apart or to identify, number them with a permanent marker.

Finding SOURCE stones in Nature

Before you set off, repeat your intention to yourself: 'I would like to find a suitable set of stones for my SOURCE work', then take a little time to go for a walk in a relaxed and internally open mood. It is also helpful if your vision is a little unfocused and you allow your perceptions to roam far and wide – the more loosely, receptively and calmly you go about it, the more easily and quickly you will find your stones. You will be surprised by what you encounter on this excursion – it's less a case of actively looking for the stones and more a case of the stones finding you, or 'calling' to you.

You are now probably wondering how you speak to stones. What I do is pause for a brief moment and direct my inner question to the stone. I then try to sense if what comes back is more a positive or a dismissive response. I intuitively feel that 'this stone wants to come with me' or 'this one, not so much'. Individual stones actually 'shine' at me from some distance away; somehow, they specifically catch my eye or my gaze suddenly falls upon them. I look down to the ground and my eyes clearly focus on a particular stone (without any conscious effort on my part!) – in short, for me, the first contact generally comes through sight. Other people tend to sense which stone suits them. Some people talk to stones; if you have ever communicated with a tree, perhaps you will understand what I mean.

So you don't have to make a great effort to look out for the right stones. Just remain relaxed and receptive and you will notice the reverse: the stones will look for you or call out to you. Rather than going out like a hunter and keeping a sharp weather eye open, simply go for a relaxed stroll, looking gently into the middle distance, and you will soon find the first stone shining out in front of you. It will almost seem as if it is gently illuminated with a beam of light, or your gaze will fall – as if by chance, but entirely unambiguously – on a particular stone. Or you will suddenly feel a physical impulse to bend down at that exact moment and reach for a particular stone lying right at your feet.

Looking for and/or finding SOURCE stones in Nature is just one option. You may already possess suitable stones, or – and this can be a real pleasure – you can visit an attractive shop and assemble and purchase a little collection of smaller gemstones (around 1–3 cm in diameter) especially for this purpose. You can either proceed much as described above to decide which stones to buy, or take individual stones gently in your hands and sense whether they want to join you in your SOURCE work. I usually use my inner voice to tell the stones how I need them to work for me.

The SOURCE process – step by step

1. Achieving the right frame of mind

Practising SOURCE means making a conscious effort to forget for a while about thinking how your current situation might be changed and your problem solved. Get into the mindset of not knowing what will happen in the next second during the course of a SOURCE session – let it arise from itself, from the SOURCE process. For the next hour, yield control to a higher power – go with the flow completely and have trust.

Asking questions of this oracle is a holy* act. Ensure there is an appropriate amount of space for the SOURCE session. Make sure you won't be disturbed while you're doing it – switch off your mobile, for example, and arrange not be interrupted by children or housemates.

Allow yourself a little time out with every SOURCE session and consciously leave the daily routine of your life behind. You might perhaps like to light a candle or put on some soft instrumental music. Have a pen and paper handy. In addition to your SOURCE stones, you will need a camera and a suitable surface on which to cast and photograph the stones. You can even swap from your rationally thinking, actively controlling, everyday mindset to a more peacefully meditative and receptive mode of consciousness during the preparations.

Before starting your stone constellation work, it is a good idea to first pause for a moment. Begin with a little prayer, or meditate in silence as best you can for a few minutes. Looking at a flower or a beautiful picture instead, or listening to calm, uplifting music, will work just as well.

Ask silently for guidance! From God, if that works for you, or from an angel, from your (or a) Master, or from your soul. You will thus

....

* 'Holy' refers to something special or venerable, and is etymologically derived from hālig, an Old English word meaning 'whole, sound, healthy' that is still found in the phrase 'hale and hearty'.
(Source: en.wikipedia.org/wiki/Sacred#Etymology, consulted 6.3.2016)

hand 'up' the reins (to a higher power) for the course of the entire SOURCE session – to the Great Spirit, as the Native Americans would say. You will notice what a relief this will bring in itself, and how beneficial it is.

Relax, as from now on you will be receiving a gift. Perhaps also take a moment to remind yourself that this method of problem-solving has been practised by shamans, medicine men and women, seers and healers all over the world in just this – or a similar – way for millennia. This is why the Native Americans always ask for the support and wisdom of their ancestors at such moments. Our forebears want to make the infinite wealth of experience they have gathered over many generations available to us as help and support.

These are nothing more than suggestions. Sense what feels right and works for you personally. Nonetheless, the important thing is for you to find a way to consciously hand over responsibility for the progress of the session to a higher power for the entire duration of the SOURCE process. This is one of the key elements in any SOURCE session. If you would like to make regular use of the SOURCE method, design a suitable ritual that gets you into the correct frame of mind so you always start your SOURCE sessions with the appropriate energy. You will find further suggestions and hints at the back of the book.

Should things occasionally become unexpectedly hard work or tiring during the SOURCE session, it is generally a good idea to remember the prayer and/or the procedure you used to begin the SOURCE session; if the process lasts much longer than an hour, the intellect and the ego unfortunately often manage to regain control.

2. Defining your subject

Choose a situation about which you would like more clarity or in which something should be changed for the better. In a few sentences, briefly summarise the subject or the situation as you are currently experiencing it. If you are able to, note down the objective of the SOURCE session, i.e. the outcome you are wishing and hoping for. If this is possible to do at this time, you will find it useful in that it further clarifies your intentions for the SOURCE session you are about to undertake; it will strengthen your inner direction.

However, often – and especially in really confused situations – such a positive vision of your goal is not achievable at the beginning of a SOURCE session. If this is the case, you need not devote any further thought to it at this point. The beautiful thing about a SOURCE session is that your goal and/or a positive vision of your eventual outcome will pop up as if by magic later on – even people who have never previously worked with positive goal formulations will find their future direction easily and clearly.

It is important that the question, subject or situation you wish to illuminate, transform or solve with a SOURCE session is close to your heart and that you have thought it through for some time in advance. The same applies for a SOURCE session as for other oracular methods, such as a Tarot card reading or casting sticks for the I Ching: the more important the question and the subject, and the more seriously you approach and entrust yourself to the oracle method, the clearer and more concrete the results will be.

The subject should not be a question you are asking out of mere curiosity or just for fun; simple yes/no questions are also unsuitable for a SOURCE session.

3. Who or what is influencing the subject?

Now think about your problem or subject and make a list of the persons and factors that influence this situation. These will be the players in the SOURCE session. They might be individuals, such as your mother, your boss or your child, for example, although groups of people can be possible players as well (such as your managers, school class, clients, team, other customers etc). They might also be qualities or character traits, such as courage, trust or honesty, for example, or inner aspects of yourself, such as your inner child, inner critic or inner saboteur. In the appendix, you will find a list of suggestions for the players that might appear in a SOURCE constellation.

The players involved will generally soon become apparent when you outline the subject and/or the problem, either out loud or in writing. Here, you should go into the subject or problem deeply enough that you are able to give an unambiguous name to the players and/or the influences involved. If you cannot do this sufficiently clearly, you will notice it later on when working with the stone constellation you have thrown. It is always possible to add in any missing important players later, however.

During a SOURCE session about a female friend of mine's divorce process, we both failed to notice for a little while that she herself was not represented in the stone constellation. There were stones for her husband and his lover, for his son, her daughter, and for their shared wealth. Everything else was represented, but she herself was missing entirely from the constellation. This was a revealing detail for her situation at the time, and this was exactly her problem; she had always been concerned about the well-being of others but had never taken sufficient care of herself. She went on to change this in her target constellation.

In the list of players, concentrate on the most important influences. If there are more than ten players, it can soon become difficult to get an overview of the stone constellation and maintaining an unhampered, intuitive flow can be considerably more challenging.

In any case, it usually becomes clear that there are only a few players whose influences lie at the very heart of the problem. This will become clear to you as soon as you skilfully change their positions; the problem constellation will lose its tension at a stroke.

4. Assigning the players to the stones

Once you have written down the list of players, select a stone to represent each one. Here again, it can be a good thing if one of the stones particularly catches your eye when you think of your boss, for example, or the stress you are feeling. You can also close your eyes and run your flat, outstretched palm over the stones to see where you are drawn. Lots of people use this method to select Tarot cards or Bach flower remedies.

Here, too, you should relax and trust your intuition. Free yourself as much as possible from all expectations. When you hold your left (heart) hand a little distance above the stones, it is very likely you will be able to sense that some of the stones feel 'different' (warmer, colder or distinct in some way) from the others when you think of a particular player. Some people even feel as if there is suddenly a vacuum pulling their hand towards a certain stone.

You can also select the stones according to colour and shape, however, or pull each in turn randomly from a little bag or container. As with everything relating to SOURCE constellation work, stay relaxed and loose and let your expectations take a back seat for a while. Place complete trust in your feelings and whatever will develop from the process. If you trust your intuition, no matter how you make your selection, it will always be the right method; you can't make a mistake here.

The good thing about SOURCE work is that you don't have to be clear at the beginning about how the individual players are interlinked with one another and/or where exactly the nub of your problem lies. It is one of the gifts of this kind of oracle work that the inner structure of the (conflicted) situation and the internal connections of the subject become apparent by themselves as you follow the steps – and you can rely on this happening every time! This is the amazing thing: the actual 'work' gets done by itself, it is 'done for you'. All you have to do is remain as relaxed and open as possible and trust the process.

In most cases, it is barely possible to remember which individual stones are allocated to which players – at the beginning of a SOURCE session, this is even an advantage, as you can then observe and analyse the stone constellation you cast entirely objectively and with absolutely no preconceptions.

Later on (in the next step), however, the assigned meaning of the stones is crucial. This is why, in addition to making a list of the players involved, it is absolutely essential to make a note of the allocation of the individual stones, so you can refer to this later on. To make sure of this, you could make a table – using the following form, for example (you'll find a template to copy in the appendix):

Stone	Player's role
Onyx	
Agate, grey	
Carnelian	
Chrysoprase	
Sodalite	
(etc)	

The set of SOURCE stones that you (always) use is entered in the first column. You can then make several copies of this table (which will already feature the stone names). The players you wish to assign at the time can then be entered alongside these.

Doing SOURCE work with other people has made me realise that (of course) not everyone knows what amber or rose quartz looks like. Working with the stone names can thus be unnecessarily tiring or even confusing. In such cases, you can introduce an additional numbering system for the stones and use it to communicate the player/stone allocations in a way that anyone can understand:

Stone no.	Stone	Player's role
1	Onyx	
2	Agate, grey	
3	Carnelian	
4	Chrysoprase	
etc		
etc		

The allocation of the stones can also be quickly recorded in a way anyone can understand with a photo:

1 Onyx, 2 Agate, grey, 3 Carnelian, banded,
4 Chrysoprase, 5 Sodalite, 6 Moonstone,
7 Rose quartz, 8 Garnet, 9 Clear quartz,
10 Unakite/Epidote-Feldspar

Fig. 8

5. Casting the initial constellation

We now come to the actual stone oracle. Working with SOURCE brings the magic of the power places used by shamans and Native Americans into your home. On your kitchen table!

a) Choosing a surface to work on

The best surface to cast your stones on is a cloth in a single colour you really like. I now own several different SOURCE cloths, as the choice of colour often varies and/or is connected with the subject. For the photo, you should ensure that your stones are clearly distinguishable from the background. I used a bright red cloth as a background for my first SOURCE sessions before changing to a white cloth (because of the photos), which I used for a long time. When I later came to review and compare my various SOURCE photos, I noticed that for me, the red background had energised the photos more powerfully from the very beginning. This is one reason you should not just try to find the most convenient way to photograph your SOURCE session;

experiment a little with various fabrics and colours until you find a background that provides the most powerful support. This may also vary with the framing of the subject. When choosing the fabric and storing the cloth, make sure it won't get permanently creased from being folded up.

I advise you to get hold of a suitable cloth (or several) to be used especially for your SOURCE work and for no other purpose. This means you will have what in coaching is known as an 'anchor'.* Just spreading out this cloth will make it easier to slip into your relaxed, unforced SOURCE state every time.

b) Casting the stones

You will now throw the first stone constellation, which will give you some clues about the interconnections or background to your subject. To do this, hold the player stones you have selected very loosely in both hands. If the stones feel much cooler than your hands, wait for a little while.

Imagine warmth and energy flowing out of your hands into the stones. Now shake the stones loosely and gently in the space between your two hands and pause for a brief moment.

Once again, consciously make contact with the stones in your hands, remembering as you do your connection with the higher power. Ask silently once again for support. Think briefly again about your subject, the thing you want to work on today, and ask that the constellation you throw will clearly reflect the current situation.

Now open your hands and throw the stones gently onto your surface. After casting the stone constellation, take a photograph as you will carry on working with the photo later.

....

* Anchoring is the process of consciously forging a link between certain triggers and reactions. (…) Anchors are used to deliberately bring about resourceful conditions. (Source: http://www.trans4mind.com/personal_development/mindMastery/anchoring.htm, last consulted 6.3.2016)

6. Interpreting your stone constellation

Now take a look at the stone constellation you have thrown: what spontaneously strikes you? Are there any noticeable gaps or large distances between individual stones, for example? Is there any extreme proximity? Are there clusters or groups that are close(r) together, or any imaginary dividing lines? Which stone is at the centre, which is on the edge?

Write down a list of the striking features. It is very likely that you won't exactly remember now what meaning each stone has and/or what role it plays; at this point this is even beneficial, as we have seen, as you will thus be able to observe and make notes entirely objectively and without interpreting a meaning in the stones.

The striking features are different in every SOURCE session. But don't worry, you will notice them straight away. I have often had the experience, for example, that one of the stones immediately falls off the table when I cast. At one SOURCE session, one of the stones even smashed into several shards when it hit the table. We first had to check its meaning, as we had lost track of it in the multitude of stones; it represented the fear of the questioner.

It has happened that someone has picked out a stone for a player's role because the stone looked so beautiful and gleaming. When thrown, this stone suddenly landed upside down, with the brilliant side underneath, and its reverse was unexpectedly plain and grey. Individual players often end up clearly distanced from the centre, while others will come together entirely harmoniously to form a (semi-) circle, triangle or other geometric shape. Many pile up so closely together that not one of them ends up in a proper lying position, or a stone may sit directly on top of another. What all this means is determined in each case by the concrete associations with your players.

Only when you have made a note in writing of all the striking features of your stone constellation should you incorporate the assigned meaning of the stones from your list of players. Here, interpretation is amazingly easy, as a rule. Sentences such as the following are generated, for example: 'Fear is lying on top of a successful business idea.' Or: 'Your heart's desire fell straight under the table.'

In one SOURCE session in which I was involved, the person doing the session was concerned about her relationship with her youngest son. The mother's fears and her stepmother lay between the two stones representing the mother and son.

By now, I think you will have an idea of how an interpretation of the stone constellation you have thrown might look; you will also find further hints and tips in the sample chapter to follow.

7. The path to your target constellation

After the interplay of the forces at work in your current situation have become more transparent with the aid of the stone constellation you have cast, the next step is concerned with finding a new, powerful and healing 'target' or 'solution' constellation.

The path from your starting constellation to a liberating target constellation: adjusting the players

To do this, you will now intuitively and judiciously change the position of individual stones in the constellation. Here, it is not a matter of going on the offensive and striving for some concrete goal by deliberately making moves that work towards a solution that you find intellectually appealing. Instead, here – and especially here! – it is important to remain unblocked and open to impressions.

At this point, simply let yourself be guided, slowly and intuitively, step by step. If you are stuck in a crisis, the problem is exactly that you yourself cannot recognise a good and suitable solution, or see potential for change that in fact is already under your nose.

'We cannot solve problems at the same level of thinking at which we created them.'
Albert Einstein

As a rule, we ourselves are completely unable to see the 'big picture' that lurks behind our circumstances. At the time, we (still) cannot recognise what opportunities and potential possibilities are hidden within this or that crisis or a particular problem. By using a target constellation that you have created intellectually and rationally, it is probable that you will considerably limit the true scope of what lies before you. Every problem wants to tell you something – it might want to make you aware of a change of course that is required, for example. These valuable hints are just waiting for you – but to reach them, 'you' and/or your ego have to take a step back and allow the solution to reveal itself to you on its own. During a SOURCE session, the deepest, truest, best and most healing influences that are currently available to you (and to all concerned in the situation) will reveal themselves, and in general these influences are greater, more far-reaching, more wonderful and yet at the same time simpler than anything you could have previously imagined.

But let's return to your SOURCE constellation: what promptings do you feel to change it, to move it around (without thinking about it for too long)? Try it out. You can only win by doing this – you have nothing to lose, as you have photographed the original SOURCE constellation with your digital camera. You can recreate it at any time.

In your opinion, what has to be changed, or moved, and to where, so that the picture becomes more harmonious, more peaceful or healthier? What would you have to alter to make you feel better while simultaneously taking the tension out of the situation?

You will now carefully rearrange individual stones, one after another, until the stone constellation has lost its tension and is released or liberated. During this time, try to keep your intellect and your ego as much in check as possible. Allow yourself to be guided by your intuition and your gut feeling the whole time.

When you have found your target or healing constellation, you will sense it. Your body, your gut feeling, your heart or your intuition will report back to you very clearly – as soon as the altered constellation is the right one, you will experience a feeling of relief.

There is often a kind of feeling of inner realisation. This sometimes happens very suddenly, after you have moved some small stone or another just a little bit further. In any case, you will find looking at and experiencing this altered image much more pleasant (in comparison with the first stone constellation).

You should proceed cautiously, allowing yourself time to move the individual stones around, as you will notice that as soon as you move even one of the stones, the aura and the energy of the entire constellation will change immediately. This may not apply to every single stone, but it will be the case with most, and as soon as one of the stones is in a different place, it may well be that the next alteration you had originally planned now no longer fits. This means that after every single alteration you must always try to sense what the next step and your next move will be.

You might perhaps be wondering what criteria you should use to make a move? There are no universally applicable rules for this, but there are two principles to go by.

One way is that you can approach it with reference to content: when there is a blockage between you and your project, for example, you can try to move this aside or even remove it entirely.

Here you should remember the second principle, however, which is always to intuitively bear in mind the vibrations and aura of the overall constellation in each and every move. It can be compared to Ikebana, the Japanese art of creating incredibly beautiful flower arrangements: using just a few flowers or blossoms, a couple of twigs and a little foliage, it is possible to enter a meditative state and create airy and inherently perfect arrangements. Here, the art consists of placing the various colours and shapes – as well as the empty space between them – at an ideal distance from – and at a perfect angle to – one another.

The process is very similar with SOURCE constellations: the over-all picture, the entire structure, the distances and the positioning of the stone with respect to one another are optically, and thus energetically, harmonised. The target constellations emanate a certain peace; an inner order that had previously fallen out of equilibrium will now have been restored.

You should always pay more attention to this second principle than to the first, the one about content. Something like this might happen, for example: you would like to move aside or even entirely remove from the pattern the *fear* that, in the constellation you have thrown, lies between you and a new project. But when you objectively and intuitively use your feelings, you notice that this is not right. You can't take away that stone as it simply belongs, both optically and energetically, as a part of this constellation. Without this stone, there is clearly something missing; the picture loses its overall balance. A comparable situation will be analysed later, in the sample session below.

Very rarely it happens that the original constellation has, after a while, been pretty much obliterated but the person feels just as little at home with the new, altered constellation as they did with the original one. This is one of the reasons you should take a photo of the first constellation immediately. If you really were to get stuck, or 'lose your way', as it were (which in my experience very rarely happens!), you can simply go right back to the first stone constellation you threw – which you have preserved with the first photo.

Take a quick break, consciously relax again, and remember that you have yielded responsibility for the alteration process to the Source. Then start again at the beginning, in absolute peace and full of trust, by altering the original stone constellation.

You can also insert additional stones into the constellation. In a difficult professional situation, for example, you could add a stone that represents something like courage, perseverance or the ability to say 'no'.

As soon as you have reached a target constellation, you will clearly recognise and feel it. Take a photograph of this altered stone constellation as well, as soon as you have the feeling that it is right and powerful for you as it now stands. Take it as soon as you sense a clear feeling of relief or of harmonisation.

What is happening here can hardly be put into words, but you will experience it during your first attempt at a SOURCE session: you feel how your entire system, your intuition, your gut feeling or your heart relaxes as if it has been set free – and sometimes this can happen very suddenly, after you have moved a little stone only a short distance. Just looking at and/or feeling your way into the new stone constellation will bring you considerable relief.

The altered, target constellation is often not that radically different from the initial constellation. This is also realistic, as you certainly don't want to turn your entire life upside down, but rather achieve your aim easily and harmoniously with the minimum of trouble. Just from its appearance and energy, the first stone constellation you throw conveys a feeling of disharmony – often without you even paying attention to its assigned meaning. As a rule, the second radiates a certain harmony, even just from its appearance. A kind of inner order has been restored here, and this is the moment the stone constellation process is complete. Now, remember to take a photo!

8. Formulating a goal statement

An outcome statement can generally be derived relatively easily from the content of the players present in the target constellation and the way that these players are lying in relation to one another in the constellation. Look at the constellation and sum up this image in a sentence, using the assigned meaning of the player stones to help you.

Always write down your goal statement. Just writing it down brings your goal, and the situation in which you are set free, one step closer to physical reality by virtue of being committed to paper. A goal vision always has greater effect when it is written down rather than just being an abstract thought in your head.

If on occasion you don't manage to find a goal affirmation, stay calm. You can still carry on working with the photos. The goal statement, the healing, liberating affirmation that underpins the process, will sometimes come later. In some cases, the message of the target constellation has suddenly arrived like a bolt from the blue a few days later. It became apparent only after the person had worked with the photos for a few days and slept on it for a few nights.

The liberating statement, the healing affirmation found in this way, was in many cases so powerful that there was no need for further work with the pictures. I remember one SOURCE session where the person in question, who was in a very difficult situation at work, kept repeating the outcome statement of the SOURCE session to herself in complete joy. She found it much easier to get through a crisis period of restructuring using the statement.

I also remember the example of a woman who did not work with the outcome statement at all. Without recalling any of the content or contexts from the SOURCE session, she restored herself to equilibrium simply by looking at the photos of the target constellation several times a day.

When you write down your target message, the message from the liberated stone constellation, please mark it with the current date and keep it safe. After a SOURCE session, changes can often come about so casually, so harmoniously, so coherently, that you fail to notice that (and indeed how) the situation has improved or rectified itself.

When formulating the outcome of a SOURCE session in a sentence, it is a good idea if the wording reflects your certainty that you will soon achieve this goal. So please don't use formulations such as, for example: 'I wish that I could become calmer.' Here, it would be better to say: 'I am/remain completely calm, no matter what is happening around me.' Or: 'I know that …' If you find this difficult to believe at first, you can also work with beginnings like: 'I am open to …' or 'I deserve to …' Imagine anchoring this belief in your whole body. Let it stream into every cell, even the gaps between your cells, and into the code of your DNA.

9. Finishing up

Gratitude has a supportive influence on the path to healing and liberation. It is an important element in any SOURCE session, as gratitude exerts a powerful force and acts like a magnet for wish fulfilment.

When you have finished, you should therefore thank all the powers that have guided, protected, encouraged and supported you in this SOURCE session. Thank your helpers, the stones, and of course, the power of the Source, which has given you an answer and shown you a new path. It will continue to support you on the next step with the photos, helping you to activate the solution you have found and realise it in your life.

It is important to round off every SOURCE session in gratitude, as this lends the whole process even more strength – not least as we demonstrate with gratitude our belief that something has really worked and will continue to work.

10. Transformational work with the photos

The transformation and improvement of your situation will now continue to develop without your consciously having to do very much about it. You can work on it with your two photos over the next few days: place the photo of the first stone constellation you cast on the table to the left (or hold it in your left hand) and place the transformed target constellation beside it to the right (or hold it in your right hand). Now glance briefly at the left-hand photo of the first constellation and shift your gaze to the right, to the photo of the target constellation, where you will briefly linger. Repeat this several times: briefly glance at the photo on the left, then shift your eyes to the second picture and pause there a little longer. Follow this whole procedure for a few minutes twice each day; that will be enough.

Your conscious input here will be minimal: using the technique described above, you will just be looking at the two photos for three minutes, twice a day for a week. The best time is first thing in the morning directly after waking up and last thing at night before going to sleep. As the photos will fit into any purse or wallet, you can of course keep them with you as a reminder and energy prop and take a quick look at them more often during the day, although only the three-minute morning and evening sessions were stipulated in the original SOURCE process. That's exactly how I do it and it works extremely well!

Among the many different people (and subjects) for which and/or with whom I have now 'SOURCEd', there have been many who have intuitively discovered their own path to working with the photos. Some put up the photos in the office where they can always see them, some concentrate exclusively on the target image.

Through your work with the two photos you will, on an unconscious level, be learning the path from the problem to the achieved goal, from entanglement and chaos to stable, harmonious order. The more days you spend working with the two photos like this, the less important the first, left-hand one will gradually become and the longer you will find yourself concentrating on the target image, without even trying to.

In addition to the work with the photos, you can also leave the target constellation itself set up on the table (if it will be safe there) for a few days to exert its influence on you.

During this time you may well forget the meaning allocated to each stone in the constellations. This will not hamper the process; the transformational work with the two images will still run smoothly, even when you are unable to remember the assigned meaning of each stone. Your eventual goal statement, which you can also use as an affirmation, is more important here. As you look at the photos, repeat your goal statement silently in your head or out loud.

If the meaning of the individual stones is important to you, mark the stones in the photos with a permanent marker. Personally, I think this makes the photo too busy and that the stone and/or energy constellation works best on its own, but try it out and see for yourself.

The two photos also form a lasting memento. They are a kind of visual receipt for the SOURCE session and the transformational and liberating processing of your problem that it achieved. I have seen many different SOURCE photos from many different people and subjects over the last few years, and I have found the majority of the target photos very touching. I experienced a feeling of correction, clarification and inner harmony from them, even though it was not my subject or SOURCE process.

Time and time again, intractable, seemingly hopeless problem situations – where those concerned were really at their wits' end – have resolved themselves completely (and as if by themselves) after a SOURCE session, often within a few days. The problems dissolved as if they had never been – so gently and naturally that it seemed to the person as if that conflict had never even existed. All this is possible and accessible for you, without you having to do very much towards it – apart from holding a one-off SOURCE session for an hour, or an hour and a half, and then looking at your constellations photos for a few minutes over the course of a few days afterwards.

To demonstrate the SOURCE method in more concrete and easily understood terms, let's have a look at a detailed description of another sample session.

Another practical example

The problematic situation

A student – let's call her Irina for the purposes of this story – had taken and passed all the exams for her degree and also completed a three-month internship at a company where she had been offered an interesting topic for her Bachelor's thesis. She had started doing some research during the internship, assembling the critical literature and reading around the topic, which she found really interesting. She had made plenty of notes and even written the first computer programs for the piece of work. Directly after her internship (and having returned to her university), she had also been able to secure one of her professors as a future supervisor for the topic.

But then, everything had suddenly come to a dead halt. She had actually only intended to take a break and relax a little for a week or two, but this had unexpectedly turned into several months. She couldn't understand how it had happened – the time had just flown by, and she hadn't even particularly enjoyed it. So she had already lost an entire term and had now just spent Easter at home with her parents, who were financing her studies.

Her relationship with her parents was good, but this last Easter holiday had become unexpectedly stressful for all concerned. Her father had set her straight about her situation in a friendly, but very definite manner, and she had consequently promised to write up her Bachelor's thesis without delay before officially submitting it to the exams office during the current term. She could well understand that her father was annoyed, as he was the one who ultimately had to finance each additional term.

With a bad conscience, but firmly resolved to finally complete her studies, she got down to work as soon as she returned to university. It was difficult, as she no longer felt able to wade through the giant pile of notes, technical articles and computer printouts. She felt she knew less than during her internship. The more she read through her notes, the more she was gripped by the feeling: 'I just can't do it! All this will never add up to a text with a proper sustained thread running through it.'

For several days, she had indeed (as promised) sat at her desk and devoted herself consistently to the topic and/or the notes she had made and the research she had done. However, the six or eight hours a day she had planned turned into two at the most. She hadn't made a plan for how she was to begin and had no idea which steps had to be completed in what order. Overall, this project suddenly seemed to her like an enormous, unclimbable mountain; whenever she got to grips with the topic, she felt swamped, like a failure. She even thought about abandoning her entire course.

When I told her about the SOURCE method, she was immediately enthusiastic and definitely wanted to try it out. I asked her to sum up her problem in a few sentences. She said: 'I can't manage to get down to writing my Bachelor's thesis even though I have firmly resolved to complete it. I have no idea why I can't get any further with it and I also don't know where or how I can carry on working on it now.'

The first stone constellation

Irina wanted to use her own semi-precious stones for the SOURCE session, along with a handful of rowanberries and some little natural pebbles she had picked up the day before on a stroll.

After a brief meditation to get into the right frame of mind for the SOURCE work, we assembled a list of potential players:

- her Bachelor's thesis, which seemed an enormous, insuperable mountain of work
- completing her degree course, with a presumable change of circumstances and location
- feelings of guilt towards her parents (because of the money)
- her father
- being confused and lacking a plan

- a clear goal with definable individual stages
- failing to 'get out of the blocks' and/or her inner procrastinator blocking her
- her interest in the topic
- the professor supervising her final thesis
- official registration of the topic with the exams office

When we came to selecting specific stones for the influencing forces involved, Irina decided to start the SOURCE session with the following players:

1	enormous, insuperable mountain of work
2	feelings of guilt towards my parents
3	what my father expects of me
4	clear work goal with definable individual stages
5	feeling that far too much is expected
6	my interest in the topic
7	official registration of the topic with the exams office
8	the screeds of unsorted, completely haphazard notes and documents on my computer

Her assignment of stones to the players looked like this:

1

2

3

4

5

6

7

8

Fig. 9. Irina's allocation of stones to the players
1: Petrified wood, 2: Amber, 3: Thulite, 4: Yellow Calcite, 5: Tourmaline, black,
6: Disthene, orange, 7: Chrome Diopside, 8: red berries

And the stone constellation she threw was this:

Fig. 10. The constellation cast by Irina

Striking patterns and positions arising

We noted the patterns using the following formulations, as neither of us could remember what content lay concealed behind the individual stones. As we saw earlier, at this point it is even beneficial to be able to observe and interpret the stones entirely neutrally and objectively.

One of the four red berries immediately rolled away under the table (never to be seen again). The red berries were otherwise arranged away from the centre and a good distance from each other.

The piece of wood, the amber stone, the black stone and the yellow stone were arranged together, almost in a line.

The orange stone and the green stone lay beneath and to one side of the line, while the pink stone lay to the other side – 'like a fork in the road', as Irina commented. She said it looked as if there was a decision to be made between one side and the other.

We then filled in the content using the player list and the assignment photo. This produced the following:

One of the many unsorted, haphazard notes and PC documents (8) disappeared immediately from view (and remained hidden). They lay at the far periphery of the constellation, and thus did not make up the centre, although Irina had thought exactly this was the case when she got these papers ready as the basis for carrying on with her work.

The enormous, insuperable mountain of work (1), the feelings of guilt towards her parents (2), the feeling that far too much is expected (5) and the clear work goal with definable individual stages (4) were arranged together in a line.

To one side beneath this line of four, there was 'what my father expects of me' (3), with 'interest in the topic' (6) and 'official registration of the topic' (7) on the other.

Irina thought that this looked like there was a decision to be made between 'what my father expects of me' on one side and 'interest in the topic' and 'official registration of the topic' on the other.

The messages conveyed by the stone constellation made immediate sense to Irina. She commented, 'The absolute crux of the whole matter is establishing my clear goal with definable individual stages. However, this is getting difficult, very difficult, for me as long as I remain as if hypnotised by the enormous, insuperable mountain of work while also feeling under pressure (including extreme time pressure) because of the feelings of guilt towards my parents – as well as simultaneously having the feeling that far too much is expected of me in the whole situation.'

'The other reason for this,' she added, 'is that I have never put together such an extensive academic text. I simply don't have the academic skills and the right work techniques. Perhaps I should make an appointment at the academic advice centre at my university?' She added in surprise: 'I'd never thought of that!'

She realised that the notes and materials she had collated during her internship were not that important at that precise moment. The focal point was instead the decision to be made about whether she wanted to continue to feel stressed and helpless because of the pressure from outside or – based on her own interest in the topic, which she had freely chosen herself, and had enjoyed choosing – to work towards officially submitting her Bachelor's thesis.

The path to the target constellation

The first things Irina instinctively removed from the SOURCE session were the three red berries. Looking at the image with the berries removed (see fig. 11) immediately helped her to relax. She had originally thought that these notes (interview notes from her internship period and from meetings with her professor, as well as the notes she made while conducting research and reading articles on the topic) would be the basis for her later work.

However, Irina's attempts to work through and organise these details had completely blocked her every time she even began to try. This was exactly what had caused her to feel: 'How is that supposed to work? I'll never manage it!'

Fig. 11. Interview and research notes (8) removed

For this reason, she was happy to accept the idea of leaving the scraps of paper to one side (at least for the moment) – in fact, it was actually a relief to her. She also thought it a good idea to approach the topic from scratch instead – using 'only' her interest in the topic and her previous knowledge from her course and her internship. During our conversation, it became clear to her that it would also be a considerable relief to her father if she were to concentrate exclusively on her personal goal from now on and confidently pursue it with a will. She therefore decided to move the expectations of her father to one side in the stone constellation for the moment.

Fig. 12. Father's expectations (3) moved to one side

The next thing she wanted to do was gradually remove from the constellation the stones representing the enormous, insuperable mountain of work, the feelings of guilt towards her parents and the feeling that far too much was expected. She found the picture far more pleasant without the enormous, insuperable mountain of work.

Fig. 13. Constellation without the insuperable mountain of work (1)

However, removing the stone representing her feelings of guilt (see fig. 14) left her with a sense that there was a gap in the constellation, as did alternatively removing the stone representing being overstretched (see fig. 15): it wasn't right, and resulted in a weakening effect on the overall constellation.

Fig. 14. Constellation without the feelings of guilt (2)

Fig. 15. Constellation as in fig. 13, but with the feeling of overwhelming expectation removed (5)

Perhaps you are even able to follow and sense that as you look at the two photos?

She also felt that attempting to remove both simultaneously made the constellation unstable.

She felt that doing this would make the influence of her father's expectation even stronger (despite the new, greater distance).

Fig. 16. Constellation as in fig. 13, but with the feeling of overwhelming expectation removed (5) and the feelings of guilt (2)

This was one of those typical SOURCE session moments in which it is a good idea to consider whether additional resources – i.e. new players, new stones – might be included in the constellation. Irina considered what might be able to help her in this process. She came back to the idea of the academic advice centre at the university and also thought of her guardian angel, in whom she had firmly believed as a little girl.

She took a smaller, dark grey stone to represent the academic advice centre and produced a guardian angel picture (which she had bought years previously at a church in Majorca) from her purse. I was once again amazed at the unusual coincidences that crop up with the SOURCE method: the little guardian angel icon that Irina wished to add to the stones in the SOURCE session featured a stream with rocks in it. The size of the stones in the picture perfectly matched that of the SOURCE session stones, so that both the academic advice centre stone and the 'clear goal' stone fitted seamlessly into the picture once she had so intuitively added her angel picture.

Fig. 17. Constellation with the new academic advice stone and the guardian angel image

This was her target constellation, which we photographed. We then took another photo of it without the stone representing her father's expectations of her.

Fig. 18. Target constellation without her father's expectations

Here, Irina wanted to experiment over the next few days to find out which of these two photos would be more consistent and empowering for her as a target image.

The message in the target constellation
Only three of the original players remained in the target constellation. At the centre lay the clear goal with definable individual stages, with Irina's interest in the topic and the looming official registration of the topic with the exams office close by.

'At her back', Irina now had a professional academic advice centre, which was a free service offered by her university, and her guardian angel, which had been with her for some time. At this point, Irina spontaneously said: 'I have all the support I need to complete my Bachelor's thesis successfully.' This neatly sums up the message in the target constellation.

To finish, we both silently thanked the powers that had accompanied and guided this wonderful process.

Irina then worked with the two photos below for three minutes, morning and evening, for three weeks:

Fig. 19

She began to feel the effect of the SOURCE session clearly only two days later, and was suddenly able to motivate herself every day to continue successfully working on her final thesis.

Now it's your turn

To try out and learn the SOURCE method for yourself, the best thing to do is to make a list of topics you would like to work on and/or have cleared up. These are just as likely to be great dreams and visions as problems, challenges, old wounds, fears or physical complaints. Get into the habit of doing regular SOURCE sessions. It works especially well early in the morning, when everything is still very quiet, or at weekends, when you perhaps have more time and leisure to spare. In addition, you should also do a SOURCE session whenever you have a feeling of 'now would be a good time!' Here too, you should follow your intuition. You will be guided in this. It is almost impossible to make a mistake in a SOURCE session. Every session will expand your inner space and enrich both your life and that of the people around you.

You can also hold a SOURCE session for other people, as long as you feel confident enough with the method. You can do this in the presence of others and also at a distance; both are possible, but you should always check that the other person would like you to. Don't be tempted to interfere in the lives of others uninvited; this won't do justice to SOURCE work. In a SOURCE session, one of the aims is to follow your life path as it is determined for you, and this requires the end of egocentric control and/or the need for mastery. This need for control is strong in a lot of people as it is based on insecurity and fear.

SOURCE for advanced users

I have learned many other things during the countless SOURCE sessions I have held or attended over the last few years, and I would like to share these with you as well.

Tips and tricks: learning from the experiences of others

When searching for your target constellation, it can be helpful to add additional supportive players to the stone constellation to give you strength – especially if you are not experiencing a clear feeling of relief or realisation. These additional resources might be a guardian angel, a power animal, protection or support (as ideas in themselves), or qualities such as courage and trust, or whatever seems to be missing from the situation. This often leads to individual, creative solutions and your treasure trove of ideas for subsequent SOURCE sessions will thus grow ever larger over time.

You can also make use of another symbol as a complementary, supportive force that may be useful in (re)solving the current situation; in the sample session, for example, it was the little guardian angel picture. A constellation can sometimes only be resolved by adding a particular object, often with great power, as was the case with a small, green jade turtle that a lady had brought back many years ago from a wonderful, once-in-a-lifetime holiday in China. For her, this turtle was a symbol of freedom and a personal reminder that it is indeed possible for dreams to come true.

In a SOURCE session with a man who was having professional problems, the quest for additional resources for his target constellation failed initially. However, as he enjoyed playing cards in his leisure time, he cried out at one point, 'A joker! I need a joker!' A joker would be a player that I personally wouldn't be too keen on, but in this case it was just the right thing. I have since suggested 'the joker' to other people on several occasions; it can clearly be a powerful resource.

In a SOURCE session with a self-employed woman looking for a new business idea, I suggested placing an additional stone for her new venture in the target constellation. 'Yes, ok,' she said hesitantly, and immediately reached straight for a very particular dark green gem. 'But…,' she then hesitated, 'the new business idea doesn't exist yet. I still have to find it. This is my problem. That's why I can't just simply add it!'

I pointed out that while this new business idea didn't exist now, it probably would in the future. It would thus already exist now on a subtle level. 'So this idea is already energetically present somewhere?! And all I have to do is reach out and grab it?!' She was relieved.

At some point during the session it became clear that the woman was looking for a perfect solution for her target constellation. Such an expectation creates enormous (and unnecessary) pressure.

Always remember you can try out even the craziest idea when looking for your target constellation. You can first add an angel to your constellation, for example, then if your feelings tell you that it's not right, you can swap it for another player.

You should consider anything and everything that helps or heals, anything that provides support or lends succour. Try it out. Then see, and/or feel, how the change works for you. Give yourself time, create inner space and take baby steps.

After the last little adjustment, does the constellation feel more powerful or more harmonious than before? What would make you feel better? You don't notice a difference? Then forget the last change. If the ultimate solution is not quite perfect, it doesn't matter. The only important thing is that you notice that a move has been made towards clarification and harmonisation, towards lifting your burden, towards relief, growth or healing; the best thing of all about the SOURCE method is that the target constellation will use the newly generated energy to turn the liberated, healed future we wish for into reality – without us consciously thinking about the topic any further.

A lot of people believe that change, healing or clarification of conflict involves great effort. The following question has often been helpful on the path to a target constellation: 'Assuming easy solutions were allowed and supposing they were possible, what would you move now?'

Troubleshooting: how to find solutions to obstacles

The SOURCE session doesn't seem to want to finish

A SOURCE session is essentially playful, often a pure joy. To this day, I am still amazed at the ease with which this profound undertaking is completed as a rule. However, I have also (albeit very rarely) experienced SOURCE sessions that I have found exhausting and a real job of work. What struck me about these was that the processes always took considerably longer than usual. Things usually flow using the SOURCE method; the work is not only easy but also amazingly quick, lasting an hour at most. I have even cast and adjusted (highly successful!) 10-minute SOURCE sessions.

Should you find that a SOURCE session is becoming tiring, something is not working out as planned.

First, be aware that stress or inner pressure will block any SOURCE session, but please don't judge yourself or the other person if you are in company. Just be aware of how you were feeling and how the process was working at that particular moment. Did you have expectations in mind? Did the other person have expectations in mind? A SOURCE session requires trust, and this means yielding to a higher power, allowing yourself to be guided – and not wanting to be at the wheel yourself. Lean back for a moment, inhale deeply and exhale a few times and consciously connect with the Source and/or the higher power that you tuned into as you started the session.

A SOURCE session becomes tiring as soon as you begin moving stones and working from your personality, from your ego. To be honest, I occasionally find myself slipping back into this old habit. Don't worry, a SOURCE session will let you know that you are doing this: it will become less enjoyable.

This is a good thing, however – as soon as you notice, you can change the mood relatively easily by pausing briefly and considering that every SOURCE session is drawn from a deeper Source and/or guided by a higher power. Consciously re-establish contact with this Source – you may have to repeat the first step, achieving the right frame of mind – and then enjoy the way that the stones and your hands are only an instrument, guided and steered by the Source itself.

'It is not your efforts but your devotion
that determines your success in life.'
Eckart Tolle

Problem working with the photos

I have rarely had feedback from someone who found it difficult to make an inner connection with the photos. When this has cropped up, it is usually because the person was looking at the photo from the wrong perspective. Have you ever turned your passport photo upside down and looked at it? It's astonishing – you can hardly recognise yourself, and the same is of course true for SOURCE photos. In your daily SOURCE reminder and activation work, you should look at the image as it was when you threw the SOURCE constellation.

Updates and feedback

'What's been happening with your subject in the meantime? What's changed?' I asked a woman with whom I had held a SOURCE session four weeks previously.

'The second photo represents my desired target situation,' she answered, 'and it does indeed connect me with it every day. It's gradually leading me closer to the point where I deserve it and I dare to choose it for myself. It's very good at helping me get used to new things, increasing the chances that it will in fact come true. It's a good – and at the same time, very easy – way of making the reinforcement of your own thoughts into a concrete image.'

Another woman said: 'You said the SOURCE session will do it all for you. At the beginning, this really shocked me, as it seemed too simple that it would all happen on its own. I had to get used to the idea first that I really didn't have to do anything myself, that something like that, such a liberating change with no effort, no active input at all, is even possible. The photos helped me a lot here; I now believe in these subtle changes in my thoughts and my belief system. I was very surprised when you asked during the SOURCE session "How would you now wish the situation to be different as a goal?", but I simply grabbed the rose quartz and laid it intuitively beside the rock crystal, without too much inner effort. Just like that – spontaneous, intuitive, quick and easy! I really couldn't imagine that something like that would work, because it was so easy to do. It was child's play. Now, two weeks after the session, I notice how it is clearer to me that this good future is possible and can happen. I now specifically recognise that this great future can only come true through change in me and I believe this future is already very close.'

The aim at another SOURCE session was to develop new, appealing products for a small company. 'Did you work towards this with the photo? And if so, how?' I enquired, about three weeks afterwards. 'I fall into resonance with the photo of my target situation and, in this state, I do indeed generate good, new product ideas. I am greatly inspired by the pictures. The photo is especially good at maintaining the link to my goal. I can take it with me wherever I go, even on a business trip. I also think it's great that the meaning of the photo is not apparent to others – unlike a poster with a goal affirmation slogan, for example; I'd never hang something like that in my office.'

SOURCE is visual alchemy

'What you focus on, expands!'

The SOURCE process is translated into images when you photograph the stone constellations. These photos will make the energy, the power, the wisdom, the comfort and the inner guidance of your SOURCE session eternally accessible to you (any time, anywhere!). Most people find a normal computer printout to be less energetic and expressive and prefer proper glossy photo prints. If you have the space for it, you can also leave the target constellation itself out for several days to continue having an effect on you.

A large part of the information we receive is transmitted visually. When you look at your SOURCE session photos, the new information and vibrations from the SOURCE session will reach you and program you a little more each day. The best times for this to happen successfully are when your reason is not as strong but your consciousness and your heart are especially open, so in the mornings directly after waking up, for example; at night, if you happen to wake up; or after a meditation. The pictures will help you to manifest to yourself the new energy, your new vision, the future you desire even if the old past is still running (down).

'My SOURCE target picture is so beautiful, I can't stop looking at it!' was the feedback from a businessman who had initially been extremely critical. Another person said: 'I had absolutely no difficulties with working with the pictures for a few minutes every day: I found it easy right from the start, and I still find it easy to stick to it every day, as I enjoy looking at the photos so much!' He had his target constellation photo in his car.

You don't need to have the assigned meaning of the stones present in your mind when looking at SOURCE photos; nor do you need to have a concrete idea of what it means for you and your life when you move internally from the first stone constellation to the second. There is also no need to know how this path in your life will look from a practical perspective – all of these things are of secondary importance, as working with SOURCE pictures speaks to you directly, on the level of your heart, your soul and your consciousness (and bypassing your reason).

In addition, it may not yet be entirely clear what is being transformed during a SOURCE session, nor exactly how this is being achieved; realisation, that 'aha' moment, might not come until a few days (or nights) later. Sometimes, it doesn't come in an intellectual, strictly rational way at all, and the function or meaning of a particular stone might even remain unclear for a considerable time. In some SOURCE sessions, a 'joker' or placeholder is introduced without being defined in detail; the process of release and resolution has begun nonetheless.

As a rule, our brains work rationally and intellectually, proceeding logically and sequentially, i.e. step by step. In this mode, they work either meticulously, with great attention to detail, or holistically, looking to gain an overview and to identify contexts in their totality. This is how we grasp works of art and pictures. We would never think of scanning a painting from top left to bottom right, pixel by pixel, detail by detail, as we do when reading a text. A lot of people mainly take in most of the information by using their eyes, while others listen; some experience their environment and/or are obliged to understand new things through actions and deeds. In the latter case, working, feeling, arranging and adjusting the stones during a SOURCE session will go a long way towards achieving clarity. Working with SOURCE photos is ideal for visually orientated people. People who learn and take in information better aurally should concentrate on working with their goal statement.

Linking into the energy of SOURCE photos

When you look at the photos of the constellations, please don't do it with a hawk-eyed, focused stare – instead, try to use a soft, relaxed gaze. Decades ago, I read somewhere how the Native Americans, when tracking for a hunt, would extend their focus and consciously expand their field of vision out to the right and left, as well as up and down. You can easily do the same if you use your hands to help you: while holding your head level and continuing to look straight ahead, angle your arms at 90 degrees and raise them until your hands are at about head height on either side of you.

As you continue to look straight ahead, you will now see each hand in the corner of your eye. Hold your hands beside your head, palms facing forward, about 30 cm from your face at approximately eye level – the pose the bad guys adopt in a Western just after the sheriff has said 'Hands up'.

As you continue to look straight ahead, you will still see your hands at the same time (this is important!); slowly, very slowly, move them backwards until you can still just see them out of the corners of your eyes. Here, it helps to waggle your fingers a little. With a little practice, you will soon be able to achieve a field of vision of about 180 degrees, i.e. you will be looking straight ahead but at the same time you will also be able to see both hands beside your head. The way you look at things will change automatically and be quite different from usual.

This is precisely the point of this exercise – changing your field of vision automatically causes an alteration in your perception of things; both your field of vision and your consciousness are being extended. Entirely automatically, your thoughts will become much calmer and more meditative during the process. Although you are certainly no longer capable of analysing the pattern of a tablecloth in this state, it is nonetheless a wide awake, present way of perceiving – you will be aware of a great deal, all at once and in a very in-the-moment way.

You will now immediately notice any movement, however small, within your field of vision, for example; this is why this mode of seeing is so suitable for hunting. You will also *feel* a lot more, in a way I cannot describe in words. It is possible to see in this extended way while simultaneously feeling yourself inhabit your whole body, right down to the tips of your toes.

Now look at your stone constellation and/or the photo in the same manner, with a broad, receptive and open gaze. Be wholly and consciously aware of your body as you look. You can also willingly open your heart if you wish. You will then naturally lower your hands – and please don't worry about whether your field of vision is still sufficiently broad. You may perhaps also find other methods (that will work consistently for you) for energetically connecting with what you see lying before you in a better and more intense way.

Here, try also to sense the space between you and the photo of the constellation, or the constellation itself; in this state you can get a sense of how all things are connected. You may perhaps also sense how what you see and the things with which you surround yourself (in your home, for example) can have a direct influence on your state of mind.

Using SOURCE on the go

A great advantage of the SOURCE method is that you can spontaneously make use of it, any time, any place, anywhere, no matter where you are, and without too much preparatory work. You can also do it without a camera; all you need is a pen and paper. You will be able to find suitable stones anywhere, even in the middle of a big city. Cast the stones and alter the constellation just as you have learned; then, instead of taking a photo, simply sketch the constellations onto paper.

If it is important to you, you can even recreate the constellation later and photograph it.

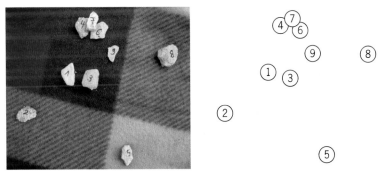

Fig. 20. You can also sketch your SOURCE constellation

Alternative ways of achieving the right frame of mind for a SOURCE session

Not everyone will be comfortable with saying a prayer, and 'meditation' is also a word that tends to put a lot of people off. In such cases, a really good alternative way to achieve the right frame of mind for a SOURCE session is to listen to gentle, meditative music in silence for a short while.

Alternate nostril breathing, as used in yoga, or a few cross-crawl exercises from the 'Brain Gym', can also be a good way in. You can look at a beautiful picture for a few minutes or, if you're sitting outside in the summer, gaze at the sky, a tree or a flower.

You can also think of an inner image that is specific to SOURCE work, perhaps a symbol that helps you personally to connect with your heart and the unity of the universe. You might imagine you are surrounded by a shining light or how the wings of an angel protect and gently cradle you.

Any little ritual that enables you to distance yourself from your everyday surroundings and consciousness by helping you to relax and enter the SOURCE process with confidence will be suitable.

The following prayers may make it easier to get into the right frame of mind:

> I ask for guidance in this SOURCE session. For the duration of the session, I shall put to one side my ego, my rational understanding, and the temptation to control everything or shape events and people according to my needs. I shall not determine what happens, I shall allow myself to be guided, listening to the voice and the guidance of my soul and/or of all the souls that are touched by this topic. May this SOURCE session be an instrument of peace and healing.

I hand over my topic, problem or project to this SOURCE session. I pray for and ask for a solution, a new drive, that casting the stones today will bring me this solution. I trust in the guidance that will show me how the stone constellation should look or feel so that I can be freed and healed and filled with light. So be it!

May the angels be with me and guide me during this SOURCE session, as they are always with me when I need help or call to them. I place my faith in the eternal power of their wingbeats, their light, their wisdom and their transformational power – Amen!

May all that arises from this SOURCE session today be the best and the greatest it can be, better and more powerful than I can ever imagine. Everything that troubles me or worries me, the reasons for this SOURCE session, I give over to this higher guidance. It will enable me to see what can be seen – to realise what can be realised – to feel and hear what can be felt and heard. It will also give me the courage and the strength, the perseverance, the patience and the devotion I need to accept the healing of this 'medicine'. Thank you!

Or inspired by Native American tradition:

Great Spirit, who has always surrounded us, ever-present and all-pervasive, in the wind, the sun, the earth, the cycle of water in Nature, in the sky above us and in the earth beneath our feet.

You live in each and every one of my cells, in my heart and in my soul.

Please give me the strength to sense you, to feel you and to hear you, along with the courage to trust and follow my inner voice with the aid of these aeons-old stones.

Great Spirit, please guide me, show me the way and help me perceive the situation simply and clearly. Untangle what has become tangled and show me a solution, an alternative that will provide enlightenment, relief and release, to the greatest benefit of all those involved. So be it!

Modification and expansion of the SOURCE method

If you have a safe place for it to sit undisturbed, leave your target constellation set out for a few days and allow it to work on your space and your life situation.

Instead of using a cloth, cast your constellations on a large piece of monochrome paper. The advantage of this is that you can record the assigned meaning of the stones on the paper right next to the stones themselves. Here, I would still always recommend taking a SOURCE photo first, before writing in the names and then taking another one with captions. This preserves the pure clarity of the constellations for when you work with the photos.

You can use a permanent marker to write each association of the stones on the SOURCE constellation photos. You can either note down their assigned meaning or just their numbers, which you can look up in the list of players.

Even the shape of the stones can sometimes be important. In a SOURCE session of my own with completely ordinary pebbles, I suddenly saw, right at the end, that the stone at the very centre of the target constellation was heart-shaped.

If your SOURCE stones are ordinary pebbles that are not so easy to tell apart, you can number them; you will then also have another way of assigning them to the players. This is recommended if you are having difficulties with assigning the stones or feeling which stone should be chosen for which aspect, for example. You can then leave the allocation of the players to chance in that you write down the forces involved in the situation one after the other in a numbered list as they occur to you, for example:

Nr.	List of relevant players
1	New role at work
2	Self-doubt: 'I can't do it!'
3	No time to settle into job
4	Discipline and perseverance
5	The team leader
6	...
7	
8	

You will instantly have an automatic and clear allocation of the stones (which have already been numbered).

You can also do a SOURCE session with another person (or with several). Once a married couple did a SOURCE session together and first both identified the list of players and then assigned the stones. One of the pair cast the stones (for both of them). They worked together to adjust the stones before working with the photos (this was done individually).

Afterword

Thank you for reading this book and allowing me to share this wonderful gift with you. I really hope that you have already done a SOURCE session and experienced it for yourself, so you can share my enthusiasm for this mystical method of consulting oracle stones and constellations!

I wish from the bottom of my heart that this fantastic tool will help you to become healed, happier, stronger and more radiant – and that, with the help of a SOURCE session, all this will happen more quickly and easily than ever before.

Please follow your heart, go your own way, follow the guidance of your soul – and follow the SOURCE stones and the valuable advice and unique answers that come from the Source.

Fig. 21: Halfway up Bell Rock (in Sedona)

About the author

Kira Klenke is a mathematician who worked as a professor of statistics for more than twenty years. She has gained a reputation for teaching statistics to people who thought it absolutely impossible that they could learn so successfully – and even with such joy – and a second vocation as a coach has grown out of her teaching duties at university.

Her interest nowadays is to help people to let go of old and obsolete life patterns and unlock their full potential. Her certification as an NLP coach and her many qualifications in the realm of spirituality enable her to work holistically in these endeavours.

Having sought a deeper meaning in life even as a child, she has been actively involved in creative writing, energy work and shamanism since 1984. She has visited power places all over the world, encountering forces that lead to the root of all things, the Source.

Feedback

I really appreciate all your feedback and I love to hear what you've experienced with the SOURCE-method.

You can reach me at kira.Klenke@googlemail.com.

If you enjoyed the book please leave a review on Amazon.

Thanks so much!!
Kira Klenke

Appendix

Questions that might help you find resources for your target constellation:

- What person (either living or dead) would you like to have helping you in this situation?
- Do you know anyone who would know exactly what to do in such a situation and so could provide support for you? It doesn't matter here if you know them personally or not – even novel characters or comic-book heroes are possible options.
- Is there anyone among your ancestors who might provide support here?
- Is there a favourite teacher, a master or some celebrity (even if you have never met them in person) who might be able to help you?
- Who would you call in the middle of the night if you suddenly felt very ill?
- What could you do or use to ease your pain, sorrow, fear, jealousy etc?
- Who would you like by your side if you wanted to talk about or celebrate an achievement or a victory?
- Who (or what) inspires or supports your greatest dreams in life and/or your heart's desires?
- What animal or what place in the natural world possesses exactly the energy, powers or abilities that you could really use here?

List of involved players: template

Stone number or name of the gemstone	Player's role

Player suggestions

From your birth family:

- ☐ Mother
- ☐ Father
- ☐ Grandmother
- ☐ Grandfather
- ☐ Brother
- ☐ Sister
- ☐ _____
- ☐ _____
- ☐ _____

From your own family:

- ☐ Wife/ex-wife
- ☐ Husband/ex-husband
- ☐ Life partner
- ☐ Daughter/son
- ☐ Granddaughter/son
- ☐ Mother/father-in-law
- ☐ _____

- ☐ _____

From work:

- ☐ Boss/superior
- ☐ Colleague
- ☐ Employer, assistant etc
- ☐ Client
- ☐ _____
- ☐ _____

Archetypes, fairy-tale figures, creatures from fables:

- ☐ Dragon
- ☐ Unicorn
- ☐ Good fairy
- ☐ Wizard (such as Merlin or Harry Potter)
- ☐ Death
- ☐ The warrior
- ☐ The wise old man/woman
- ☐ The hero(ine)

- ☐ Hercules
- ☐ Aphrodite
- ☐ Elf
- ☐ _____
- ☐ _____

From your leisure time, neighbourhood, circle of friends, a spiritual community:

- ☐ Friend
- ☐ Spiritual master
- ☐ Neighbour
- ☐ Club member
- ☐ _____
- ☐ _____
- ☐ _____
- ☐ _____

Players associated with health:

- ☐ Doctor/healer
- ☐ My illness

- ☐ Part of my body
- ☐ A medication
- ☐ A behaviour
- ☐ Therapy
- ☐ Operation
- ☐ My powers of self-healing or convalescence
- ☐ Healer
- ☐ _____
- ☐ _____
- ☐ _____

Players of the psyche:

- ☐ My fear
- ☐ Inner child
- ☐ Inner critic
- ☐ My sorrow
- ☐ Inner procrastinator
- ☐ Loneliness
- ☐ Inner saboteur
- ☐ Self-confidence

- [ ] Life vision
- [ ] Wishes/desires
- [ ] Courage
- [ ] My creativity
- [ ] My jealousy
- [ ] The compliant goodie-goodie
- [ ] The rebel
- [ ] My power/strength
- [ ] _____
- [ ] _____
- [ ] _____
- [ ] _____

From your energy system:

- [ ] A particular chakra
- [ ] Your aura
- [ ] _____

Spiritual beings, animals, power places, masters:

- [ ] Dog, horse, cat, etc
- [ ] Power animal/spirit guide
- [ ] Angel
- [ ] Master
- [ ] Jesus/Dalai Lama
- [ ] God/Great Spirit
- [ ] My role model
- [ ] A crystal or mountain
- [ ] The ocean
- [ ] Favourite place in Nature
- [ ] Ancestors or forebears
- [ ] _____
- [ ] _____
- [ ] _____
- [ ] _____

Groups of people:

- ❏ Clients
- ❏ Family
- ❏ Neighbourhood
- ❏ Work colleagues
- ❏ Management/ executive board
- ❏ School class
- ❏ _____
- ❏ _____

New resources for the target constellation:

- ❏ A particular book
- ❏ A particular song
- ❏ A colour
- ❏ A scent
- ❏ A particular Tarot card
- ❏ An element (water/earth/ fire/air)
- ❏ A Bach flower
- ❏ A joker
- ❏ Someone who advises/ protects you
- ❏ _____
- ❏ _____

Anything you can
imagine belongs here;
allow yourself to be creative.

notes

notes

notes

notes

notes

notes

Have you ever heard that small skeptical voice piping up in your head when you are trying to think positively? We all experience this, it is our mind or ego.

Learn how to 'trick the mind' and create effective affirmations to attract the positive into your life with Askfirmations.

Chris Alexandria
Askfirmations
Make affirmations more effective
by using powerful questions
Paperback, full colour throughout, 96 pages
ISBN 978-1-84409-693-0

This powerful book with its beautiful dragon illustrations allows you to enter the mystical world of dragons. Once you are ready, it will help you to get to know your own dragon, your close personal companion, and to share its invincibility, wisdom and magic.

Christine Arana Fader
The Little Book of Dragons
Finding your spirit guide
Paperback, full colour throughout, 120 pages
ISBN 978-1-84409-670-1

This handy reference book explains how to find relief from headaches, colds and fear of flying, and will help you to cope with long car journeys or lengthy days at your computer, all with just a few reflex zone massage strokes. You'll never want to be without your helpful companion!

Ewald Kliegel
Reflexology Made Easy
Self-help Techniques for Everyday Ailments
Paperback, full colour throughout, 80 pages
ISBN 978-1-84409-666-4

There are so many occasions on which to send our best wishes to those close to us and choosing the correct stone gives those wishes added power and emphasis. This handy little book is fully illustrated with charming photographs and reveals the appropriate stone for each occasion and its message.

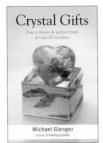

Michael Gienger
Crystal Gifts
How to choose the perfect crystal
for over 20 occasions
Paperback, full colour throughout, 96 pages
ISBN 978-1-84409-665-7

Healing Crystals is a comprehensive and up-to-date directory of 555 healing gemstones, presented in a practical and handy pocket guide format. In the revised edition of his bestseller, Michael Gienger, famous for his pioneering work in the field of crystal healing, describes the characteristics and healing powers of each crystal in a clear, concise and precise style, accompanied by four-colour photographs.

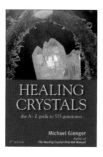

Michael Gienger
Healing Crystals
the A – Z guide to 555 gemstones, 2nd edition
Paperback, full colour throughout, 128 pages
ISBN 978-1-84409-647-3

Powerful yet concise, this revolutionary guide summarizes the Hawaiian ritual of forgiveness and offers methods for immediately creating positive effects in everyday life. Ho'oponopono consists of four consequent magic sentences: 'I am sorry. Please forgive me. I love you. Thank you.' By addressing issues using these simple sentences we get to own our feelings, and accept unconditional love, so that unhealthy situations transform into favorable experiences.

Ulrich Emil Duprée
Ho'oponopono
the Hawaiian forgiveness ritual as the key
to your life's fulfilment
Paperback, full colour throughout, 96 pages
ISBN 978-1-84409-597-1

This is an easy-to-use A-Z guide for treating many common ailments and illnesses with the help of crystal therapy. It includes a comprehensive colour appendix with photographs and short descriptions of each gemstone recommended.

Michael Gienger
The Healing Crystal First Aid Manual
A practical A to Z of common ailments and illnesses and how they can be best treated with crystal therapy
Paperback, with 16 colour plates 288 pages
ISBN 978-1-84409-084-6

Adding crystals to water is both visually appealing and healthy. It is a known fact that water carries mineral information and Gem Water provides effective remedies, acting quickly on a physical level. It is similar and complementary to wearing crystals, but the effects are not necessarily the same.

Gem Water needs to be prepared and applied with care; this book explains everything you need to know to get started!

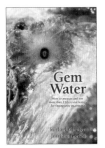

Michael Gienger, Joachim Goebel
Gem Water
How to prepare and use more than 130 crystal waters for therapeutic treatments
Paperback, full colour throughout 96 pages
ISBN 978-1-84409-131-7

First edition 2016
The Miracle Problem-Solver
Kira Klenke

This English edition
© 2016 Earthdancer GmbH
Editorial and translation:
JMS Books llp, www.jmswords.com

Originally published in German as:
Das Sedona-Stein-Orakel
World © 2015 Neue Erde GmbH,
Saarbruecken, Germany
All rights reserved.

Book jacket photography:
Frédéric Prochasson/fotolia.com
Design: Dragon Design, Elbe

All photos © Karola Sieber,
www.makrogalerie.de
with the exception of page 2, 7, 71 and
77: Kira Klenke; 6: soapysoft/fotolia.
com; 7: Wendy/Wikimedia Commons;
78: Anita Jakim; 4/5: Paul Moore/
fotolia.com

Design & Typesetting:
Dragon Design, Elbe
Set in Janson Text

Printed and bound in China.

ISBN 978-1-84409-698-5

Published by Earthdancer GmbH,
an imprint of:
Findhorn Press, 117–121 High Street,
Forres, IV36 1 AB, Scotland.
www.earthdancerbooks.com
www.findhornpress.com

FSC
MIX
Paper from
responsible sources
www.fsc.org
FSC® C011223

Consult our catalogue online (with secure order facility) on
www.findhornpress.com
Earthdancer Books is an Imprint of Findhorn Press.
www.earthdancer.co.uk

EARTHDANCER

A FINDHORN PRESS IMPRINT